Mapping Our World

by Janine Scott

Content and Reading Adviser: Mary Beth Fletcher, Ed.D.
Educational Consultant/Reading Specialist
The Carroll School, Lincoln, Massachusetts

Spyglass
BOOKS

✷ COMPASS POINT BOOKS

Minneapolis, Minnesota

Compass Point Books
3722 West 50th Street, #115
Minneapolis, MN 55410

Visit Compass Point Books on the Internet at *www.compasspointbooks.com*
or e-mail your request to *custserv@compasspointbooks.com*

Photographs ©: Tony Arruza/Corbis, cover; Two Coyotes Studio/Mary Foley, 4, 8, 9, 10, 11, 12, 13 (inset), 14, 15, 20, 21; TRIP/H. Rogers, 5, 16; PhotoDisc, 5 (inset), 7; NASA/Corbis, 6; MAPS.com/Corbis, 13; TRIP/D. Brooker, 17.

Project Manager: Rebecca Weber McEwen
Editor: Heidi Schoof
Photo Researcher: Image Select International Limited
Photo Selectors: Rebecca Weber McEwen and Heidi Schoof
Designer: Erin Scott, SARIN creative
Illustrator: Anna-Maria Crum

Library of Congress Cataloging-in-Publication Data

Scott, Janine.
  Mapping our world / by Janine Scott.
      p. cm. — (Spyglass books)
Includes bibliographical references and index.
  ISBN 0-7565-0362-0
  1. Cartography—Juvenile literature. [1. Cartography. 2. Maps.]
  I. Title. II. Series.
  GA105.6 .S36 2002
  372.89'1044—dc21
                        2002002748

Contents

World Maps

Maps can show us many things. They can show roads, cities, the stars in space, and even the shape of the land.

A star map

Did You Know?

A globe is a ball-shaped map.
It is shaped like Earth.

Map Patterns

Maps often show us patterns. Water moving in the oceans and the shape of the land make patterns. Sometimes these patterns change slowly. Sometimes they change quickly.

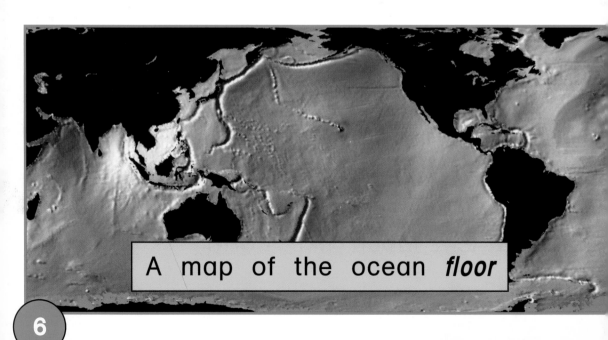

A map of the ocean *floor*

A hurricane

Did You Know?

Weather maps show where weather is, such as a *hurricane*. Weather maps can change quickly.

Near and Far

Street maps help us find an address in a certain area. Road maps show how to get from one place to another. They show cities, roads, and highways.

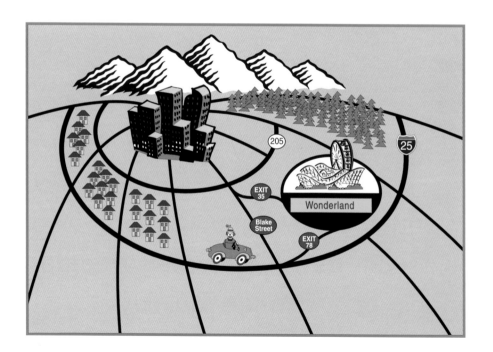

Did You Know?

Businesses print small street maps on their *catalogs* and fliers to help people know how to find them.

The Key to the City

The key to reading a map is just that—a key! A key has **symbols**. An airplane symbol shows where an airport is. A blue line is the symbol for a river.

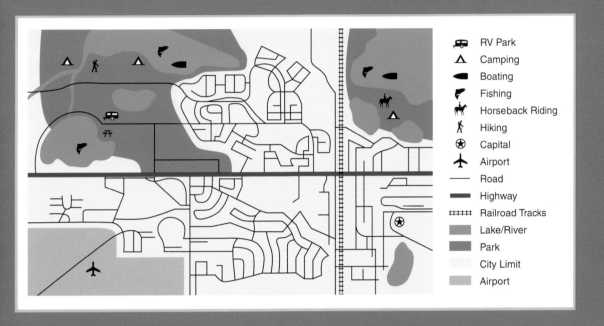

RV Park
Camping
Boating
Fishing
Horseback Riding
Hiking
Capital
Airport
Road
Highway
Railroad Tracks
Lake/River
Park
City Limit
Airport

Did You Know?

A railroad symbol looks like a train track.

Railroad Tracks

Map Math

To read a map, you need to know the size of the piece of land the map is showing. This is called the scale. A large-scale map shows a small area. A small-scale map shows a large area.

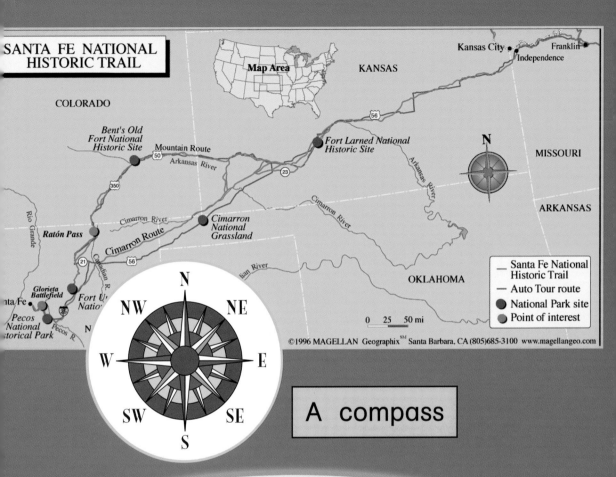

SANTA FE NATIONAL
HISTORIC TRAIL

Map Area

KANSAS

Kansas City
Independence
Franklin

COLORADO

Bent's Old
Fort National
Historic Site
Mountain Route
50
Arkansas River

56

Fort Larned National
Historic Site

N

MISSOURI

350

23

ARKANSAS

Cimarron River

Rio Grande

Ratón Pass

Cimarron Route
21
56

Cimarron River

Cimarron
National
Grassland

Arkansas River

Canadian R.

lian River

OKLAHOMA

Glorieta
Battlefield

nta Fe

Fort U
Natio

25

Pecos
National
torical Park
Pecos R.

0   25   50 mi

©1996 MAGELLAN Geographix℠ Santa Barbara, CA (805)685-3100 www.magellangeo.com

— Santa Fe National
    Historic Trail
— Auto Tour route
● National Park site
● Point of interest

N
NW   NE
W   E
SW   SE
S

A compass

Did You Know?

To show directions, maps often use
a ***compass***. Some compasses have
16 points.

Imaginary Lines

Lines that run across and down a map or a globe help us find any place on Earth. Latitude lines run across a map. Longitude lines run from top to bottom.

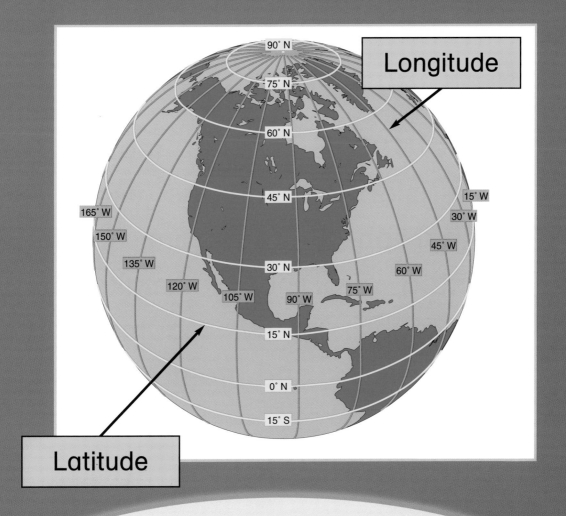

Longitude

Latitude

Did You Know?

Using latitude and longitude numbers, you can find any place on Earth.

The Mapmakers

In the 1900s, making maps got easier. Mapmakers used photographs taken from newly invented airplanes to make their maps. Today, mapmakers use *satellites* and computers.

A photograph from an airplane

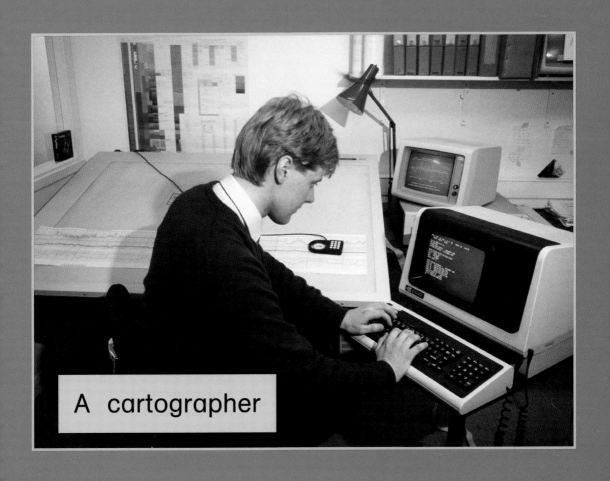

A cartographer

Did You Know?

People who make maps are called cartographers.

Fun Facts About Maps

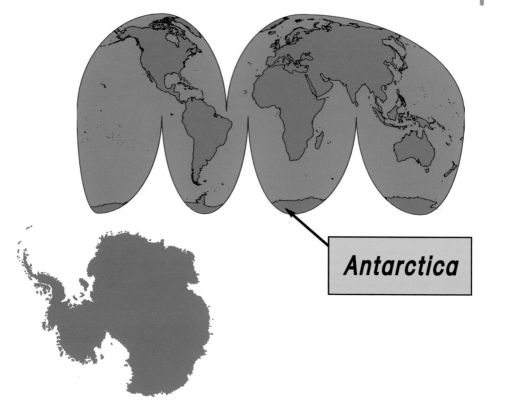

Antarctica

How Antarctica is really shaped

A flat map is not as correct as a globe. Earth's land doesn't look the same when it is flattened out.

The word "atlas" is a Greek word.

In Greek stories, Atlas was a giant who carried the world on his shoulders.

Today, an atlas is a book of flat maps.

Make a Pirate Map

You will need:

- markers or colored pencils
- paper

1. Draw landmarks such as islands, rocks, and caves.

2. Add a scale and a compass.

3. Color your map.

4. Write clues for a pirate partner
   to find the treasure you
   have hidden!

Glossary

Antarctica–a continent at the south end of Earth

catalog–a booklet that shows the things a company sells or does

compass–a tool that shows directions

floor–the very bottom surface

hurricane–a storm with high winds and lots of rain. Hurricane winds swirl around in a big circle.

satellite–a machine that flies around Earth

symbol–a picture that stands for a word or idea

Learn More

Books

Chambers, Catherine. *All About Maps.* Illustrated by Dave Cockcroft. Danbury, Conn.: Franklin Watts, 1997.

Knowlton, Jack. *Maps & Globes.* Illustrated by Harriet Barton. New York: Thomas Y. Crowell, 1985.

Royston, Angela. *Maps and Symbols.* Austin, Tex.: Raintree Steck-Vaughn, 1999.

Web Site

mapsplanet.com

Index

GR: H

Word Count: 205

From Janine Scott

I live in New Zealand, and have two daughters. They love to read books that are full of fun facts and features. I hope you do, too!